LIFE, THE AMAZING STORY

PART OF THE RAINBOW OF LIFE'S SECRETS SERIES

BY

TORRY FOUNTINHEAD

AIRÉ LIBRÉ PUBLISHING & COMPUTING LTD.

For more information contact:

Airé Libré Publishing & Computing Ltd.

Suite 306 , 185-911 Yates St.

Victoria BC V8V 4Y9 Canada

Tel: 1-250-592-3099.

Http://www.al.bc.ca

info@al.bc.ca

Published by:
Airé Libré Publishing & Computing Ltd.
http://www.al.bc.ca
Book Design © Torry Fountinhead

ISBN-10: 0-9781498-1-5
ISBN-13: 978-0-9781498-1-9

Life, The Amazing Story
ISBN-10 0-9781498-1-5
ISBN-13 978-0-9781498-1-9
51799

9 780978 149819

THE RAINBOW OF LIFE'S SECRETS SERIES

This series is bringing to our children, young and old, a variety of stories about life, with symbolic pictures to feast the eye, as the variety of colours of the rainbow in the sky; to denote how life is varied, never boring, and always justifies an adventurous spirit.

We might have more than just the seven colours of the rainbow represented within this series of books, but are we not all of several hues and shades?

May the books inspire both young and old, and bring joy to your hearts.

IV

Life awoken feeling the excitement

Of so much to do and so much to learn

Evolve to be a dream-come-true

To have a worthwhile story

Life has taken a walk

Thinking now that it started

Will it have an end?

If yes, then when? How?

But Life got busy living
And the questions were put
In the back of it's mind
And Life marched on forward

At first, it all seemed to flow

Endless moments, come and go

But then Life noticed patterns

And started to anticipate cycles

Beautiful dawn in crisp colours

Followed by bright day of sunshine

Busy skies in pale blue

Were the canvass for the dancing clouds

Evenings came with magnificent sunsets

Bringing forth, starry nights

All became quiet and calm

For night asked Life to rest

Dreams ensue, and Life wondered

Was it awake, or just on another plane

It wondered at the stories

And was eager to learn

There is so much to ponder

And so much to see

Yet, Life loved the quiet

A moment just to be

When Life came about again
It felt a force within
Calling it to movement
What direction to?

Then Life felt its power
It could stream anywhere
It can stream through anything
And be whatever it will dream

Life felt large and wondered

Can it be anything it wanted?

Can it be in more than one thing?

Can it be in more than one form?

At first, Life enjoyed streaming about
With no aim, no goal
But Life quickly got bored
And looked around for more

Life chose first to fly about
Than entered a planet
Within it found a pulsating rhythm
And a dance was created

Life rotated in an endless swirl

Around the sun, with friends about

Dancing in the endless space

Full of wonder and delight

It started asking questions
But heard no answer
It asked again, and then
Felt a stirring desire

Be Life, as what you want
Feel, experience, see, and grow
Be big or small, you'll never change
As you are made to last for evermore

Given the permission – being allowed

Life discovered its own imagination

With it, Life weaved possible stories

All testing its power to see

17

Life discovered that seeing
Outwardly, or inwardly
Allows it to plan, and feel
What it can be in all ways

Life suddenly understood
It all depended on the theme
Of the initial intent
Invented for each story

But Life had no experience, as yet

And wanted so much to feel

That it set out to try it all

Although it was all an unknown

When an idea created a good experience
Life got exhilarated, and wanted more
When another idea brought pain or sorrow
Life remembered the good that was

21

Life felt its power again

And concentrated even more

On better ideas, scenarios, and more

To see a lot before, and know

Life discovered inner knowing
And listened within to whispers
Feeling it how would it all go
So it may choose the road

23

Sometimes it knew good and bad would follow

The bitter and the sweet are joined

And then Life discovered the rose

Showing beauty, wonder, and thorn

Life remembered the promise

Of being eternal, creative, and strong

So Life forgave itself for the pain and sorrow

And marched on with the creative glow.

What dreams are you weaving?

www.ingramcontent.com/pod-product-compliance
Lightning Source LLC
Chambersburg PA
CBHW041431090426
42744CB00003B/37